THE KING WHO WC

AND OTHER KINGS

By B. A. Ramsbottom

2003

Gospel Standard Trust Publications
12(b) Roundwood Lane, Harpenden,
Hertfordshire AL5 3DD

© B.A.Ramsbottom 1999

ISBN 1 897837 21 6

Reprinted 2003

Printed by
OlivePress, Stotfold

Note by the author

This book originated as a series of talks to my Bible class (young people in their teens and early twenties). Hence the style in which the book is written, and its purpose - to be of spiritual help to young people. Writing the book has brought back happy memories of our meetings.

I would emphasise that, though primarily intended for young people, I trust the book will be profitable to older ones also.

B.A.Ramsbottom
November 1999

CONTENTS

A Look At The Kings 5

Table Of The Kings Of Judah 6

The King Who Would Not Listen
    Rehoboam 7

The King Who Prayed
    Asa 12

The King Who Could Not Say No
    Jehoshaphat 17

The King Who Was Influenced By Others
    Joash 26

The King Who Proved A Disappointment
    Amaziah 31

The King Who Became Proud
    Uzziah 36

The King Who Walked Humbly Before His God
    Jotham 42

The King Who Trusted God
    Hezekiah 46

The Most Wicked King
    Manasseh 55

The King Who Obeyed God's Word
    Josiah 60

A LOOK AT THE KINGS

The question is sure to be asked: what have all these Old Testament kings to do with us? Amaziah? Joash? Jotham? Who were they? Can there be any profit for young people today in considering the lives of these men who lived nearly three thousand years ago? Surely, we live in a different world, with different ideas, different thoughts, different problems.

There are two answers to this:

1. God has said, "All Scripture is given by inspiration of God, and is profitable" - ALL Scripture, and that includes the lives of these ancient kings.

It is a sad fact that many people (old and young) know only parts of the Bible; there are many parts to which they are strangers. There are more characters in the Old Testament than Noah, Abraham, Joseph, Moses, David, etc.!

Incidentally, the lives of some of the lesser known kings are extremely interesting - in some places even exciting.

2. There are so many profitable lessons to be learned - by young people. So many of the problems these kings had are the very problems that face our young people today. You may say, "But there is no comparison between days when the fastest way to travel was by horse and now when Concorde can be the other side of the world in a few hours." Yes, but people travelled then (though much more slowly) for the same reason they travel now: for food; for love; to make war; to visit, etc.

Above all man is the same and God is the same; man in his great need as a sinner, and God in His holiness and majesty, and also in His love and mercy.

So we shall find many things that come very close to us today, that speak to our hearts, and many things that will be a real help in our problems and perplexities. Because it has never been easy for girls and boys to live the Christian life, and it is certainly not easy today.

KINGS OF JUDAH
Before Christ

Rehoboam	975 - 958
Abijam	958 - 955
Asa	955 - 914
Jehoshaphat	914 - 889
Jehoram	889 - 884
Ahaziah	884 - 883
(Athaliah)	883 - 877
Joash (or Jehoash)	877 - 838
Amaziah	838 - 810
Uzziah (or Azariah)	810 - 758
Jotham	758 - 742
Ahaz	742 - 727
Hezekiah	727 - 698
Manasseh	698 - 643
Amon	643 - 641
Josiah	641 - 610
Jehoahaz or Shallum	610
Jehoiakim or Eliakim	610 - 599
Jehoiachin or Coniah	599
Zedekiah or Mattaniah	599 - 588

The kings whose names are in *italics* are not dealt with in the following chapters largely because we are told little about them. After Josiah we have the captivity - when Jerusalem was captured and the two southern tribes taken captive to Babylon for seventy years.

There is a slight variation in the dates as given by different authorities. This follows Edersheim, *Bible History of the Old Testament*, the Oxford and Cambridge text book on 1 and 2 Kings, and the Authorized Version.

THE KING WHO WOULD NOT LISTEN

REHOBOAM 975 - 958

You can read about Rehoboam in 1 Kings chapters 12 and 14, verses 21 to 31, and 2 Chronicles chapters 10, 11 and 12.

Who was Rehoboam? He was the son of Solomon. Up till Rehoboam's reign there had been three kings of Israel - Saul, David and Solomon. But in the reign of Rehoboam the kingdom split into two: the ten tribes in the north (now known as Israel) and the two tribes in the south, Judah and Benjamin (known as Judah).

The kings we are looking at were all kings of Judah - some good, some bad. Sadly, there was not one good king of Israel. Rehoboam was the first king of Judah.

Solomon had had his faults. He enjoyed great prosperity but his rule was too heavy and taxation too severe. No one likes high taxes!

But what old Solomon could do, young Rehoboam could not do. What wise Solomon could get away with, unwise Rehoboam could not get away with.

THERE IS AN IMPORTANT LESSON HERE.

For instance, an old pastor well-established, dearly loved, can do things that would not be tolerated in a new, young pastor. He needs to walk carefully.

A church some years ago had a most gracious and most capable deacon (he was a solicitor) - so much so that they were happy to leave everything in his hands. But when he died, his successor, a much less able and gracious man, found that the church in no way would allow him the same freedom.

The King Who Would Not Listen

When Rehoboam became king he received a very courteous and sensible request - to lessen the burdens. *He would not listen.* He acted unwisely - proudly - harshly.

Always listen to a sober, sensible request. Perhaps you young people will one day be pastors, ministers, deacons, church members, parents, holding important positions in business, etc. Be prepared to listen.

Rehoboam answered in very intemperate language - very, very clever language. He said his little finger would be thicker than his father's loins! He said his father had punished them with whips; *he* would punish them with scorpions!

Avoid "clever" words. Avoid intemperate language. It does no good. It was Rehoboam's own father who had written, "A soft answer turneth away wrath: but grievous words stir up anger" (Proverbs 15. 1).

As a result the terrible split took place - the ten tribes breaking away and making Jeroboam king.

GOD'S SOVEREIGNTY IS A GREAT MYSTERY.

We read (2 Chronicles 10. 15): "the cause was of God" - why the ten tribes revolted. We have the great mystery of divine sovereignty and human accountability.

The Word of God looks beyond second causes. But this does not lessen man's sin. *Rehoboam was at fault.*

Of course, the greatest instance of this is the cross of Christ. It was God's everlasting purpose that His dear Son should die on the cross for the salvation of His people. But those who crucified Him were dreadfully guilty. Peter on the Day of Pentecost said: "Him, being delivered by the determinate counsel and foreknowledge of God, ye have taken, and by wicked hands have crucified and slain" (Acts 2. 23). God's purpose ... man's wicked hands.

Recently a young girl asked me this question. "Why did God place the tree of life in the Garden of Eden if He knew Adam would sin?" The problem of the existence and origin of evil has harassed the minds of philosophers and theologians down the ages. But one thing is clear: God will be glorified even through the entrance of sin into the world.

Rehoboam

ONE MISTAKE CAN HAVE LASTING EFFECTS

2 Chronicles 10. 19: "to this day." The division that took place, the result of Rehoboam's sin, continued for centuries, right up to the captivity.

We do need to be very careful how we behave because one slip, one mistake, can have such far-reaching effects. In Jeremiah 15. 4 God threatens great judgments on Jerusalem because of what Manasseh, King of Judah, had done many years before - and even though he repented of it!

There has been a little village chapel where for years a loving, quiet, gracious witness has been maintained to the gospel. Then there is some scandal. And perhaps a hundred years faithful witness is spoiled.

We need to pray the Lord to keep us. We need to walk carefully. Do you know the little verse?:

> "With caution we should tread,
> For as we sow we reap,
> And oft bring mischief on our head,
> By some unwary step."

The New Testament says, "Walk circumspectly." An old preacher illustrated this by the way a cat, walking along a wall with many pieces of broken glass on it, carefully puts its feet down.

Rehoboam (wisely?) decided to bring back the ten tribes to submission. But God sent a prophet, Shemaiah, to tell him not to do so. (A brave man - the army was assembled ready for battle!)

And Rehoboam obeyed (2 Chronicles 11. 4). Was he a good man after all? It is not easy to admit we are wrong, not easy to submit when God says, No.

We then read of a very wise policy (verse 5 and the following verses), Rehoboam building and strengthening cities throughout Judah, making them "exceeding strong."

We also find an exodus of priests and Levites from Israel (verses 16 and 17), coming to Jerusalem because they could not worship God freely and according to His revealed order in the northern tribes. *This strengthened Rehoboam and Judah.*

We are reminded of the Huguenots (French Protestants). In 1685, following the revocation of their right to worship freely in France, thousands fled to England. Many of them were very godly, gracious people, and many of them were very skilful craftsmen. This greatly strengthened England.

We read that Rehoboam (and Judah) walked in the ways of the Lord *for three years* (verse 17). The next chapter begins with a most sad statement: "When Rehoboam had strengthened himself, he forsook the law of the Lord."

It seems that when Rehoboam was weak or in trouble, he sought after God for His help; but when he was strong and things went well, he forgot God. *How like us!* Beware of a fair-weather religion! When you are in trouble you pray, but when things go well, prayer is neglected and God forgotten.

There was an old proverb (seemingly written by a Welsh epigrammatist):

> "God and the doctor we alike adore,
> But only when in danger, not before;
> The danger o'er, both are alike requited,
> God is forgotten, and the doctor slighted."

SIN ALWAYS LEADS TO SORROW

Chapter 12, verse 1, tells us that Rehoboam forsook God. Verse 2 tells us that Shishak, King of Egypt, came against Rehoboam with a vast army - and the Word of God gives the reason: "because they had transgressed against the Lord." Again the same prophet was sent from God (verse 5): "Thus saith the Lord, Ye have forsaken Me, and therefore have I also left you ...." (The same point as before: God looks beyond second causes.)

Remarkably (verse 6) the king and the princes "humbled themselves; and they said, The Lord is righteous."

WHEREVER THERE IS REPENTANCE, GOD IS MERCIFUL.

When the Lord saw that they humbled themselves (verse 7), He said, "Therefore I will not destroy them." *The Lord is very merciful and gracious.*

Remember in the life of Ahab, the apostate King of Israel, even when he made some weak, empty profession of repentance (1 Kings 21. 25-29), God honoured it and Israel did not suffer in his lifetime. How much more so the humble repentance of a true believer - forgiveness, salvation, heaven!

> "Come then, repenting sinner, come;
> Approach with humble faith;
> Owe what thou wilt, the total sum
> Is cancelled by His death."

WAS REHOBOAM A CHILD OF GOD?

In chapter 12, verse 11, we find that Rehoboam is still religious. He still "enters into the house of the Lord." He still worships the true God.

Only God knows whether our religion is real or not. A young lady whose funeral I was to take, not long before she died said to me, "It is not what you will say about me that matters. It is what the Lord thinks about me."

We need to be right in God's sight, born again of the Holy Spirit, prepared for heaven, blessed with repentance and faith, washed in the Redeemer's blood. *Rehoboam was not right.*

God will always have the last word, and God's last word about Rehoboam is (verse 14) "He did evil, because he prepared not his heart to seek the Lord." *He was never right at heart.*

This is the thing that really matters. This is the vital point. May we not be like Rehoboam, "the man who would not listen." Yet he *did* listen - sometimes. But he never listened to God on the vital point of his soul's salvation.

> "Am I made a *real* christian
> Washed in the Redeemer's blood?"

THE KING WHO PRAYED

ASA 955 - 914

You can read about Asa in 1 Kings chapter 15, and 2 Chronicles chapters 14, 15 and 16.

Asa is a most interesting king. He was Rehoboam's grandson. Not least he is remembered for his prayer. He is one of the good kings. He was probably only about eleven when he became king.

Though he was only young, he began to reform Judah. He put things right that were wrong.

None are too young to know and fear the Lord; none are too young for what they know to be right.

It is not easy to stand. It was not easy for Asa. It is not easy now. Young people find so many problems - at school, at work, at college. If you try to stand - not doing things on Sundays, not going to the pub, not going to nightclubs - sometimes people today will not even understand what the point is. You may be persecuted. Or people may smile at you - and it is hard to stand a smile. Many people who can stand persecution, even to blows, cannot stand being laughed at.

Your first day (at school, college, work) will not be easy. But God is able to make you stand. That is a good word: "I will lift up mine eyes unto the hills, from whence cometh my help. My help cometh from the Lord, which made heaven and earth."

But Asa *was* king - which helped. He was in a position of authority. He had the opportunity, and he took it. If you are in a position of influence - teacher, parent, "boss" - take the opportunity to use the influence for good. It is always easy to say, "Don't bother. Leave things as they are."

HOMOSEXUALITY

1 Kings 15. 12: "He took away the sodomites out of the land." "Sodomites" is the old name for homosexuals.

The Bible is always up to date. Homosexuality is one of the issues of the present day. Years ago it was never mentioned. If heard of, it was abhorred. But now not only do we constantly hear and read of it, but we have homosexuals in prominent positions: in Parliament, in the Government, ministers in the Church of England, etc.

There is this terrible lowering of standards. Not long ago Sir Rhodes Boyson said he had never heard of such a thing till he was in the navy - and then he thought the people who were telling him about it were just joking. He could not credit that there was such a thing.

The Bible speaks most solemnly against homosexuality as sin in the sight of God.

See especially the closing verses of Romans chapter one, which speaks very solemnly of this sin of homosexuality. It is an interesting fact that two or three of the kings of Judah put down this sin, and they are specially commended for it.

IDOLATRY

Asa forbade idolatry.

1 Kings 15. 13 he removed Maachah his mother from being Queen because she was an idolater. (It would appear from careful reading of Scripture that she was the Queen Mother.)

There is an important principle here. What do you do? It is a friend, or a close relative, who has acted wrongly. Do you excuse them? Or do you have to disagree, even if it is someone you love?

Partiality has worked havoc in our churches (as has prejudice also). "Yes, but he is a nice man ...." If a thing is wrong, it is wrong; if it is right, it is right - no matter who has done it. We need to remember that it is before the Lord.

However - do not fall into the sin of disloyalty, or deserting a friend if he has acted wrongly!

The King Who Prayed

Things went well with Asa. There was great prosperity. Then trouble. Often just like that with us! A vast army of a million Ethiopians, led by Zerah, with 300 chariots was coming against Asa. This was a great trial. It seemed like certain death, and destruction, and defeat.

What did Asa do?

He looked not at the things that were seen, but the things that were unseen (2 Corinthians 4. 18). He did not look at Zerah, and the million soldiers, and the chariots. He looked to his God, whom he knew was almighty.

His prayer is recorded, and it is one of the beautiful prayers of Scripture. He cast himself on his God.

ASA'S PRAYER (2 Chronicles 14. 11)

1. "Asa cried." Not just prayer - a cry. There is something very real, very urgent about a cry. "He will be very gracious to thee at the voice of thy cry."

2. He saw that God is omnipotent. The most impossible thing with Him is easy. "Lord, it is nothing with thee to help, whether with many, or with them that have no power." The One to whom we pray is almighty.

> "With heaven and earth at His command,
> He waits to answer prayer."

3. He cried for help. "Help us, O Lord." His prayer was very simple.

We think of the little prayer, "Lord, help me." It is our daily, hourly prayer. We can never wear it out. Have you had to pray it today?

4. He was completely dependent. He realised how weak and helpless he was, and depended completely on the Lord: *"We rest on Thee, and in Thy name we go."*

> "We rest on Thee, our Shield and our Defender;
> We go not forth alone against the foe;
> Strong in Thy strength, and in Thy keeping tender,
> We rest on Thee, and in Thy name we go."

ASA

This is the right attitude for a girl or boy facing problems, facing dangers, facing the unknown way. Some young people have chosen this hymn for their wedding.

5. The Lord did everything. Prayer was answered. There was a complete deliverance. Do we know the value of prayer?

The best of men are only men at best. In 2 Chronicles 16, many years later, we find Asa faced with a similar difficulty. The King of Israel was coming now to fight against him. (How sad that Judah and Israel should be at war!)

This time Asa acted as badly as he had acted well before. He went as far as to take the treasure from the house of God and send it to the King of Israel. He trusted in "an arm of flesh" instead of trusting in God.

It seems very, very strange. He fell in the place where he was strong. A man of prayer - the same circumstance - but no prayer this time! We need to be very careful *where we are strong*. Solomon was the wisest man who ever lived - but no one acted more foolishly; Samson the strongest - but no man more weak; Job the most patient - but what impatience! "Let him that thinketh he standeth take heed lest he fall."

God sent a faithful prophet, Hanani, to rebuke King Asa. He was a faithful man. But his rebuke contains a "hidden gem":

"The eyes of the Lord run to and fro throughout the whole earth, to shew Himself strong" on our behalf.

LAST DAYS - NOT BEST DAYS!

Asa's last days were not his best. Sadly, this is often true today; many of our godly old people prove that their last days are *not* their best days. (This has become a well-known prayer among us: "Let their last days be their best days.")

We do need upholding and keeping to the end. "Hold Thou me up, and I shall be safe."

Verse 10. Asa was in a rage because he was rebuked. How do we go on when someone tells us our faults? Our best friends are those that do, kindly and lovingly. Some of our best times at chapel will be when the preaching finds us out and shows us where we are wrong.

The King Who Prayed

"Faithful are the wounds of a friend."

Verse 10. He oppressed the people. It almost seems like a character change. Can this be the same Asa who prayed that beautiful prayer?

Verse 12. He was diseased in his feet (was it gout?): "Yet he sought not to the Lord, but to the physicians."

This is not a condemnation of doctors or medicine. God uses both. But we are to look to the Lord, not to the doctor. Use the means, but do not rely on them. The best means, without the Lord, will not avail; the weakest means, with the Lord, will. (We should not speak like this: "I'll take you to the doctor to make you better.")

What then was Asa's fault?

1. He was swallowed up by his infirmity. Beware of being completely swallowed up with your illness or your trouble. In the parable of the sower, when the Lord Jesus spoke of the thorns that strangle the growth, He spoke of "the cares of this life" - not just pleasures and riches. We cannot escape the cares of this life, but we should seek not to be swallowed up by them. God has prescribed a remedy: "Casting all your care upon Him, for He careth for you."

2. There wasn't much prayer. "He sought not to the Lord." Watch your spirit when in trouble and there is not much prayer.

You may say, "But this is about old people!" Young people need grace to continue, grace to endure to the end. A warning!

"SOVEREIGN GRACE O'ER SIN ABOUNDING"

Was Asa a child of God? He certainly acted badly in his last days. But God has made it abundantly clear in a wonderful word of love and mercy: "Nevertheless the heart of Asa was perfect all his days."

It is the heart that matters. Am I right at heart? And God, who knows all things, knew that Asa was. "Where sin abounded, grace did much more abound."

THE KING WHO COULD NOT SAY NO

JEHOSHAPHAT 914 - 889

You can read about Jehoshaphat in 2 Kings chapter 3, and 2 Chronicles chapters 17 to 21.

There is no doubt that Jehoshaphat was a good man - but he was unable to say NO. Right through his life we find him compromising. One of the hardest things for a girl or a boy is to say, No; to be different. But, through grace, it is a lesson to be learned. We must not be like the chameleon which changes its colour according to its surroundings. There are too many "spiritual chameleons" about. Do not be a chameleon.

So there are two things we trace right through Jehoshaphat's life:

1. He compromised. Though a good man he acted wrongly by not saying, No, when he should have said, No.

2. Despite all this, God was very gracious, and whenever Jehoshaphat was in trouble and prayed, God always answered him. How wonderful is the grace and mercy of God!

2 Chronicles chapter 17 gives us a remarkable picture of King Jehoshaphat's godliness and prosperity:

"The Lord was with Jehoshaphat, because he walked in the first ways of his father David, and sought not unto Baalim; but sought to the Lord God of his father, and walked in His commandments, and not after the doings of Israel. Therefore the Lord stablished the kingdom in his hand ... and he had riches and honour in abundance. And his heart was lifted up in the ways of the Lord" (verses 3-6). What a wonderful picture! Then we come to chapter 18.

The King Who Could Not Say No

I. THE BATTLE AGAINST SYRIA
Jehoshaphat's compromise

"Jehoshaphat had riches and honour in abundance, and joined affinity with Ahab" (verse 1). The first downward step! Ahab, King of Israel, was a dreadfully wicked monarch. Jehoshaphat even married his son Jehoram to the equally wicked daughter of Ahab and Jezebel, named Athaliah. Later we shall see the havoc this woman Athaliah caused.

Though this friendship with Ahab was bad, Jehoshaphat's language was disgraceful: "I am as thou art, and my people as thy people" (verse 3). So the two decided to go together in battle against the Syrians to recover Ramoth-gilead.

However (verse 4), it seems clear that Jehoshaphat's conscience began to prick him. He requested "enquiring at the word of the Lord" (verse 4). The present day equivalent is: "Let's have a word of prayer first." Beware of this! A word of prayer will not make wrong things right, neither can we ask God's blessing on what is contrary to His Word.

When the four hundred prophets came and said, "Go!" and, "all will be well!" Jehoshaphat knew the difference from a prophet of the Lord, and so he asked for "a prophet of the Lord." Reluctantly a most godly man, Micaiah, was sent for, and Ahab could say nothing good about him. The false prophets with exaggerated language and dramatic symbolism assured the two kings that all would be well, and Micaiah was advised to use his common sense and talk as they talked. His godly answer still rings down the ages, the standard for every true servant of the Lord:

"As the Lord liveth, even what my God saith, that will I speak."

Micaiah is one of the long cloud of faithful witnesses. Despite threats and scorn he faithfully predicted what would be the outcome - the nations scattered, and Israel bereaved of its king.

One of the false prophets, Zedekiah, smote Micaiah upon the cheek (verse 23), and so he walked in fellowship with his Lord and Master. But O Jehoshaphat! Can you really be a child of God? To remain silent when one of the Lord's servants is persecuted for the Lord's sake? "And the King of Israel and Jehoshaphat King of Judah sat either of them on his throne, clothed in their robes." All this from

JEHOSHAPHAT

Jehoshaphat not saying, No, at the beginning. The little children's hymn says:
> "The way to ruin thus begins,
> Down, down like easy stairs."

So the battle began. A treacherous friend Ahab proved to be - *he* went in disguise, but Jehoshaphat in his royal robes, so that the enemy would ignore Ahab and seek to slay Jehoshaphat. A real friend is of great value, but there is nothing worse than an unfaithful friend. Do be careful who your friends are.

God's mercy

Now see a child of God in trouble - trouble which he had completely brought upon himself and fully deserved. And Jehoshaphat knew it.

The enemy thought Jehoshaphat was Ahab. They gave commandment not to fight with any, small or great, only the king - that is, to join all their forces to slay the king (i.e. Jehoshaphat whom *they* thought was Ahab). In other words, Jehoshaphat was facing certain death, a whole army trying to kill one man. See a child of God in trouble.

"And it came to pass, when the captains of the chariots saw Jehoshaphat, that they said, It is the King of Israel. Therefore they compassed about him to fight" (verse 31). No way of escape! The end!

Now see the wonderful mercy of God:

"BUT JEHOSHAPHAT CRIED OUT, AND THE LORD HELPED HIM; AND GOD MOVED THEM TO DEPART FROM HIM."

But how great is the mystery of divine sovereignty! When God has a purpose to fulfil, it must be fulfilled, both in judgment and mercy. No one knew which one *was* Ahab; he was disguised to appear like any other soldier. But one of the enemy "drew a bow at a venture"; in other words what we would call "a chance aim" or "just a random shot." And God directed the arrow so that King Ahab was killed. So Micaiah, the prophet of the Lord, was right after all. The majority are not always in the right. God's Word will stand even if there are 400 false prophets who deny it. A very important principle as week by week we read of the onslaughts of religious leaders against the truth.

"*Call upon Me in the day of trouble; I will deliver thee.*"

Jehoshaphat proved this beautiful verse to be true. We wonder if it was a verse he knew? But it is still true today. "Call upon Me in the day of trouble" - even trouble you have brought upon yourself, even trouble you know you deserve.

"But Jehoshaphat cried out" - that wonderful *but*; and how much real prayer there is in a *cry*. "He will be very gracious to thee at the voice of thy cry."

God is a great Deliverer, and Jehoshaphat proved it. He was to prove it again.

THE SEQUEL

In chapter 19 we have the sequel to this. "Jehoshaphat the King of Judah returned to his house in peace" (verse 1). Ahab did not. But Jehoshaphat had sinned, and though the Lord had shown so much mercy, it was time for a reproof.

"And Jehu the seer went out to meet him, and said to King Jehoshaphat, Shouldest thou help the ungodly, and love them that hate the Lord? therefore is wrath upon thee from before the Lord" (verse 2). And Jehoshaphat fell under it, and amidst it all he still had the assurance of God's favour and love (verse 3).

We are constantly failing and sinning, and it is a wonderful mercy when God corrects us. Some of our most profitable times at chapel are when the Word finds us out and shows us where we are wrong. It is exceedingly solemn if we are acting wrongly and God does *not* reprove us. "He is turned to his idols, let him alone."

After that, we find the fear of God prevailing in Judah, judges being appointed, and the witness that they acted faithfully. Jehoshaphat's counsel to the judges is needed just as much by us today:

"Thus shall ye do in the fear of the Lord, faithfully, and with a perfect heart" (verse 9).

II. THE BATTLE AGAINST MOAB

In 2 Kings chapter 3 (strangely the only mention of Jehoshaphat in

Jehoshaphat

the Book of Kings) we have Jehoshaphat going into battle again, and in trouble again. And again - because he would not say, No.

This time it was Ahab's son, Jehoram, another wicked king. The King of Moab, who each year paid rich tribute to the King of Israel, had rebelled. Naturally Jehoram wanted to win back his allegiance, and so prepared to go to war with him. To make sure of victory, he asked Jehoshaphat to help though there was no reason at all why he should. It seems almost incredible: Jehoshaphat acted just as he had done before. Another evil alliance! Another failure to say, No! And unbelievably the very same words: "I am as thou art, my people as thy people," and this time, even "my horses as thy horses."

We wonder, will Jehoshaphat never learn? Has he a short memory? One thing is clear: *he is bound for more trouble.* (There is even a brief mention of another evil alliance right at the end of his reign - 2 Chronicles 20. 35).

The trouble

Quick plans were made - no mention of God - to go through the wilderness of Edom. And surely all is well, for the King of Edom joins them, making victory sure.

"And they fetched a compass of seven days' journey: and there was no water for the host." After seven days' march, the three kings and their armies were about to die of thirst. God will always have the last word, and if His children sin, He will always chastise. God's children cannot sin cheaply.

The poor King of Israel could only speak the language of despair (verse 10) but Jehoshaphat remembered "the sinner's sure retreat," his God. He asked if there were some prophet of the Lord to counsel them and help them, and unbelievably there was Elisha! We wonder whatever the prophet Elisha was doing going to battle with them. From his point of view we can only think that it was with a desire still to be a witness to God's people, even when they were acting wrongly. From Jehoshaphat's point of view, surely it was the kind providence of God.

Now see the three kings "going down" to Elisha - not summoning him to them. There are many cases in Scripture where God's servants have been honoured in the midst of trouble - for instance, witness Paul in Acts chapter 27 (the shipwreck) taking charge of the situation. But it was a withering word for wicked Jehoram: "What have I to do with thee? Get thee to the prophets of thy fathers .... Were it not that I regard the presence of Jehoshaphat the King of Judah, I would not look toward thee" (verse 13 and 14).

Then we find a most strange thing happening. Elisha said, "Bring me a minstrel." Whatever are we to make of this? A terrible crisis, three armies about to perish, and the prophet is asking for someone to come and play a tune to him! I believe the explanation is simple. The Old Testament was a dark dispensation. There was not the same liberty and access in prayer. The equivalent under the gospel would be to sit down quietly with the Word of God in prayer, seeking God's help, not rushing into things. No doubt it would be a Psalm the minstrel would play and sing. But the message is very plain to us. In any sudden crisis, do not wildly rush to do what you think best. Call on the Lord for help, and ask Him to show you what to do. "I will lift up mine eyes unto the hills, from whence cometh my help. My help cometh from the Lord, which made heaven and earth."

The deliverance

Then Elisha gave a gracious answer from the Lord. In every case, Jehoshaphat received divine help, despite his sin, when he called on the Lord. The answer was a strange one: "Dig ditches all over the valley." How often God's way is a mysterious way; but it is the right way, and the only way, and it avails.

Next morning all the ditches were full of water, sufficient for the three armies to drink, and live. God's wonderful fulfilment of His promise to supply His people's need - despite their sin. "Jehovah-jireh: the Lord will provide."

But God's wonderful answer worked two ways. The Moabites, seeing the early morning sun shining on the water in the ditches, thought it was blood. They surmised that the three armies had destroyed one another. Really, without preparation, they rushed headlong into battle: "Moab to the spoil!", only to be repulsed and defeated, even being smitten when they had retreated back into their own country.

All we can say is: what wonders God can do! Another wonderful deliverance.

III. THE BATTLE AGAINST AMMON, MOAB AND MOUNT SEIR

In 2 Chronicles chapter 20 *again* we find Jehoshaphat in trouble, and again the Lord miraculously delivered him. And this time we have given to us the beautiful prayer that he prayed.

This time it does not seem that trouble came through any particular fault of Jehoshaphat. When we see God's people in trouble, we must never assume it is because of backsliding or unconfessed sin. (If trouble comes to us personally, we should enquire of God if it *is* because of backsliding or unconfessed sin.) Many times God's people are walking tenderly in His fear when trouble comes.

The trouble this time was that a great army was coming to fight against Judah, "a great multitude from beyond the sea" (verse 2). There were the Ammonites and the Moabites, and they were joined by the people of Mount Seir. "Then there came some that told Jehoshaphat ...." We never know what we may hear, suddenly, unexpectedly. Not one of us know what we may hear even today, or tomorrow, that will throw us into turmoil. To Jehoshaphat it seemed certain death and destruction for him and for his people. So what did he do? He cast himself on the Lord in prayer. The whole of Judah gathered together "to ask help of the Lord" (verse 4). It is accounts in Scripture like this which are such a help and encouragement to us today, for God is the same.

JEHOSHAPHAT'S PRAYER

We have this beautiful prayer recorded, a "pattern prayer." Perhaps the question may be asked: in such an extremity, is it not best just to cry out? to say something like, "Lord, save us"? Is there any need for such arguments? One of the Puritans has answered that question like this: if a tiny child cries, his father is pleased to listen and help; but if one of his grown-up children comes seeking help, he likes to hear a few reasons why.

1. Jehoshaphat viewed God's omnipotence, that He is almighty,

that He can do all things. "Art not Thou God in heaven? and rulest not Thou over all the kingdoms of the heathen? and in Thine hand is there not power and might, so that none is able to withstand Thee" (verse 6). It is a wonderful help to prayer when by faith we can view who God is, and that He is "able to do exceeding abundantly above all that we ask or think."

2. He remembered what God had done for His people in past days (verse 7). He had driven out the heathen; He had given the land to His people. It is a great encouragement when we can remember how the Lord has helped us in the past in our extremities, and because He is eternally the same, to believe He will not fail to help us now.

"He who has helped me hitherto
Will help me all my journey through."

3. He remembered the temple (verse 8). Perhaps this seems strange to us, but the temple meant so much to the Old Testament saints. For instance, Daniel and Jonah both looked to the temple in their time of need. Why? Because in the temple was a high priest, a sacrifice, a mercy seat sprinkled with blood - all pointing to Christ. So in our prayers, as sinners to look to Christ and see the blood-sprinkled mercy seat, the encouragement for a sinner to venture despite all his guilt.

But more: he remembered Solomon's prayer of intercession (verse 9) for the people of God when in such a dangerous condition. "Behold, a greater than Solomon is here." In our time of need we look up to an exalted King and Priest, the Lord Jesus Christ, ever interceding for His people.

And Jehoshaphat did not forget "Thy name" (verse 8), nor do we - the name of Jesus, the sinner's all-prevailing plea.

4. He put *everything* into the Lord's hands (verse 12), confessing his utter helplessness and weakness, his complete lack of wisdom, but looking only to the Lord. None ever perished there. What a help this beautiful verse has been made to the people of God in their time of need: "We have no might ... neither know we what to do: but our eyes are upon Thee"! In New Testament language, "Looking unto Jesus."

Jehoshaphat

GOD'S ANSWER

First, God sent a prophet to encourage Jehoshaphat: "Be not afraid nor dismayed by reason of this great multitude; for the battle is not yours, but God's" (verse 15). Sometimes God speaks a word of comfort while we are still in the middle of trouble.

Directions what to do followed: "Tomorrow go ye down against them" (verse 16), and promise of sure success: "Stand ye still, and see the salvation of the Lord with you ... fear not, nor be dismayed ... for the Lord will be with you" (verse 17).

So in verses 18 and 19 we see Jehoshaphat and all Judah rejoicing. Their circumstances were *exactly* the same; their trouble was *still* as great - but now they had God's word that all would be well.

The deliverance

There was nothing Jehoshaphat and his men needed to do. God did it all. Really, He performed a miracle. As the people sang praises to their God, their enemies began to fight among themselves and destroy one another (verse 23 and 24). There were only two things for Judah to do:

1. Praise and bless God - so that the place was called the Valley of Berachah (the valley of blessing) (verse 26).

2. Gather in the spoil (verse 25), riches and precious jewels, so much that they were three days in gathering it all.

So Jehoshaphat and God's people did not lose through their trouble; they were enriched. Often it is so with God's people: they learn so much in their trials, and come out spiritually enriched. So it was with the Lord's disciples on both occasions when it seemed certain their boat would be wrecked on the Sea of Galilee. "What manner of Man is this?" "This is the Son of God." Bitter trials, but they learned more about the Lord Jesus than ever they had known before.

> "For the wonders He has wrought,
> Let us now our praises give;
> And, by sweet experience taught,
> Call upon Him while we live."

THE KING WHO WAS INFLUENCED BY OTHERS

JOASH 877 - 838

You can read about Joash in 2 Kings chapters 11 and 12, and in 2 Chronicles chapters 22, 23 and 24.

We often say that "truth is stranger than fiction" - and never was this truer than in the early life of Joash. Was there ever a prince who had a more exciting life? So as we look at King Joash, his life is not only profitable but fascinating - and extremely sad.

So what about Joash?

BACKGROUND

We must go back to Joash's great-grandfather, Jehoshaphat, the good king who "could not say No." Judah suffered for years because he compromised. You remember he did a very foolish thing: he married his son Jehoram to a most wicked woman, Athaliah, the daughter of wicked Ahab and Jezebel.

The old story is well-known of the good apples put in the dish with the rotten apple. And one by one they all went rotten. The good apples did not make the rotten one good. We are warned against bad friendships, bad marriages, bad associations - "the unequal yoke."

So it is not surprising that Jehoram turned out a wicked man. As soon as he became king he cruelly slew all his brothers. He caused the people to worship the god Baal. In a word, he overthrew all the good his father had done.

He was a miserable, wicked king. As a judgment from God, he suffered for two years from an incurable disease. At last "his bowels

JOASH

fell out."

He was king only eight years. The Bible tells us he "departed without being desired."

His son Ahaziah (Joash's father) now became king. (Jehoshaphat -> Jehoram -> Ahaziah -> Joash.) But only for one year. The evil influence of his mother Athaliah was evident. The Bible says, "His mother was his counsellor to do wickedly."

After a year he was murdered.

This is the sad, squalid background.

So we come to the exciting life of Joash - and there are three absolute distinct parts to his life: birth to 7 years; 7 to 30; 30 to 47, when he died.

JOASH (0 - 7)

As soon as Ahaziah was dead, the cruel queen-mother Athaliah massacred all her grandchildren, the royal house, and seized power herself. A vile monster! She herself reigned for six years as queen.

It was a dreadful reign. The worship of the false god Baal was encouraged. The temple of the Lord was desecrated. "Unclean" persons took over. The precious treasures were taken from the temple.

What seemed worst of all, though, it appeared that God's promise had failed! His purpose was overthrown! All the house of David destroyed!

BUT (and this is the wonderful thing!) one baby prince had escaped - Joash. The high priest's wife, Jehoshabeath (actually she was the sister of the dead king) had kidnapped the baby and smuggled him away. At first she hid him in the bedlinen cupboard, and then secretly took him to the temple. Here he was brought up as one of their own children by Jehoshabeath and her godly husband Jehoiada, the high priest.

And no one knew. The wicked old queen had no idea what had happened (and, of course, she never visited the temple!).

We see here the wonderful power and providence of God - delivering, answering prayer, bringing to safety, accomplishing His purpose. None of God's purposes can ever be overthrown, however impossible it seems.

But especially "THE SCARLET THREAD" could not be broken. Whatever was the scarlet thread? The promise made by God that one of David's descendants would be the promised Messiah, the Saviour, the Son of God. But it *appeared* there was no descendant of David, that they had all been exterminated.

Never had "the scarlet thread" seemed more precarious. What of God's promise? What of God's purpose? What of the Messiah? Had Satan triumphed? *It was the nearest Satan ever came to triumphing.*

But God's promise cannot fail. There was a baby prince still alive, hidden from sight in the temple. On so brittle a thread did God's everlasting promise hang.

And so the little boy Joash was graciously instructed in the truth in the temple.

Jehoiada. Just a word about Jehoiada. He is the first person actually to be called "the high priest." He was a most godly, gracious man - one of the outstanding characters of the Old Testament. We wonder why he is so little known?

JOASH (7 - 30)

As little Joash approached the age of seven, there was a most daring plot to pronounce him the rightful king. This was organised by Jehoiada - though he was over 100 years old!

In both Kings and Chronicles we are given the details of the plan. To us these seem rather complicated and difficult to follow. But what seems to have happened is this. Jehoiada engaged on his side the priests and Levites, the army, and the leaders of the people. Careful plans were made for the day. The soldiers were divided into three groups. The temple was kept shut up - till suddenly the young prince was brought out and proclaimed the rightful king.

Consternation followed. The old queen looked out and screamed, "Treason! Treason!" but she was taken away and put to death. The people were delighted; they were weary of Athaliah. And everything was done constitutionally!

Notice that though Jehoiada felt that this was God's will, and knew

Joash

it would succeed, yet still he made the most careful plans. *A belief in predestination and God's providence is not fatalism.* We heard of a teenage girl who prayed hard but did not work, and then was shocked when she failed her exams!

What a story Joash could have told of his remarkable beginnings! One of the most interesting and exciting parts of the Old Testament.

Joash now appeared as the perfect king. He reigned wisely and well. He leaned hard on Jehoiada, who most wisely advised him.

Not only so: there was a wonderful reformation. The temple was repaired. Baal worship and idolatry were put down. True worship was restored.

Many details are given of how plans were made to collect money for the temple. Again, these are rather difficult to follow (and also to see what is the point). There was much activity, the Levites travelling throughout the land, but little accomplished. Then a simple remedy was thought of: *a big box in the temple with a hole in the lid.* The people put in their contributions, and immediately there was enough. The money came. The temple was repaired (it had suffered through Athaliah's wickedness). Even so there was plenty left over - so vessels for the temple were purchased.

What does this teach us? Often something simple is far better than something complicated - especially in the church of God, and especially with God's blessing. Also, we need to beware of procrastination when God has a work for us to do.

Well, then, Joash - what a wonderful king! BUT -

JOASH (30 - 47)

The old priest Jehoiada died. And then we read a dreadful statement:

"Joash did that which was right in the sight of the Lord *all the days of Jehoiada the priest.*"

Now a terrible change! His religion died when Jehoiada died. Now a wicked king, an ungodly king. HE WAS A PERSON COMPLETELY UNDER THE INFLUENCE OF OTHERS.

The King Who Was Influenced By Others

Now when the people asked for the restoring of idols, he agreed. (Why did they want idols? An easier life.)

Joash now restored idolatry. He gave away the treasures of the house of God. God sent the priest Zechariah to reprove him for his sin. (He was the son of Jehoiada, so he would have been brought up like a brother to King Joash.) But Joash had him cruelly killed. His last words were: "The Lord require it." The Lord Jesus made special mention of the murder of Zechariah in Matthew 23. 35 and Luke 11. 51. This is the only hint at Joash's reign in the New Testament.

From this time, not surprisingly, everything went wrong. The Syrians invaded. Joash was plagued with "great diseases." All this was the judgment of God (2 Chronicles 24. 24). "Be not deceived; God is not mocked: for whatsoever a man soweth, that shall he also reap." At last Joash himself was murdered by his own servants.

What a sad end to a most promising life! He was only 47. He was not buried in the sepulchre of the kings. (Jehoiada was - though a priest, not a king.)

* * *

We see the tremendous importance of influence - good influence, and bad influence.

Joash was like the chameleon we mentioned previously - the little creature that changes its colour according to its surroundings. *Do not be a chameleon.* Joash changed colour according to what company he was in. This is one of Satan's temptations, but may the Lord give us grace to strive against it.

Often when a godly pastor dies, the religion of many of his congregation dies with him. So with a godly father or mother - or husband or wife - or even a son or daughter.
"Am I made a real Christian,
   Washed in the Redeemer's blood?"
Seek to be a *real* Christian. Joash never was. He was never right at heart, never right in the sight of God.

THE KING WHO PROVED A DISAPPOINTMENT

AMAZIAH 838 - 810

You can read about Amaziah in 2 Kings chapter 14, and 2 Chronicles chapter 25.

Amaziah! What are we to make of him? Was he right or was he wrong? Was he a good king or a bad king? Matthew Henry says "he was none of the worst of kings and none of the best." The Bible puts it very clearly (2 Chronicles 25. 2): "He did that which was right in the sight of the Lord, but not with a perfect heart."

The church of God is plagued with such people today - undecided Christians; not definite; half-hearted; no commitment; not in the world and not out of it. Do seek to be delivered from this, seek that there might be something *clear* in your religion.

OBEYING GOD

Anyway, there were some good things. When he became king, he put to death those who had murdered his father, but he spared their children. He was fair; he was just; but above all his action was clearly guided by the Word of God. Deuteronomy 24. 16 gives clear instructions how to act in a situation like this, and Amaziah followed it implicitly: "The fathers shall not be put to death for the children, neither shall the children be put to death for the fathers: every man shall be put to death for his own sin."

There is a vital principle here: IF THE WORD OF GOD SAYS, YES, WE MUST DO IT; IF THE WORD OF GOD SAYS, NO, WE MUST NOT DO IT. This is what Scripture means by "trembling at the Word" - not being frightened of it but treating it with awe and reverence, and seeking that our lives might be governed by it. The chief example of this in Scripture, of course, is Moses: so often we read, "As the Lord said unto him, so did he."

We must keep to this principle. Often people say, "But I am making it a matter of prayer." If God has spoken and revealed His will, there is no need to make it a matter of prayer. People say, "I am seeking God's will in it." But God will never guide you contrary to His Word. This covers so many things that concern young people.

An interesting illustration is that of J. C. Philpot. He was a minister in the Church of England, and his conscience was condemning him all the time. He knew he was doing things that were wrong - administering the Lord's supper to an adulterer and a suspected murderer; pronouncing a new-born baby when sprinkled "an heir of God and an inheritor of the kingdom of heaven"; burying in sure and certain hope a man who denied the Christian faith. But Philpot kept praying to know God's will. He received no further light, and at last the Lord showed him that all the light he needed and would receive was the certain knowledge that he was acting contrary to God's revealed will in Scripture. So he had to come out.

We are also reminded of William Huntington. One day his family were starving and he stumbled upon a bird sitting on its eggs. What should he do? Would it be cruel to take the eggs and the bird? Should he just take one? Most remarkably there is a scripture right on the subject, and the Lord brought it to his remembrance: "If a bird's nest chance to be before thee in the way in any tree, or on the ground, whether they be young ones, or eggs, and the dam sitting upon the young, or upon the eggs, thou shalt not take the dam with the young; but thou shalt in any wise let the dam go and take the young to thee; that it may be well with thee, and that thou mayest prolong thy days" (Deuteronomy 22. 6, 7).

But so much for this vital principle, obedience to Scripture; and now to return to Amaziah.

Above all there is one incident in Amaziah's life when he *really* honoured the Lord. "Them that honour Me I will honour." Very briefly what happened was this. Amaziah felt he must go to war against the inhabitants of Edom and Mount Seir. To be sure of success, he hired the Israelite army at the vast price of 100 talents. (120 years ago the authority on Jewish Bible history, Edersheim, said that if they were silver talents, they would have been worth £40,000 *then*; if gold, infinitely more.)

A godly prophet was sent (2 Chronicles 25. 7) to rebuke him and to call him to break off this unholy alliance, because God was not with Israel. And Amaziah listened. He was not offended, but was willing to do all that the man of God said. But he had a worry - the colossal loss of all the money he had laid out. "What shall be done about all this money? It will be lost." How clear God's reply by the prophet: *"The Lord is able to give thee much more than this."*

Again there is a vital principle here. NONE EVER LOSE WHAT THEY GIVE UP FOR JESUS' SAKE. If our religion is real, there are many things we shall have to give up. It may be a close friendship. If our religion never costs us anything, then it is worth nothing.

Young people today, as always, who seek to follow the Lord are called to give up much for Jesus' sake, "choosing rather to suffer affliction with the people of God than to enjoy the pleasures of sin for a season." But no one ever really lost by denying himself, taking up his cross, and following the Lord. "The Lord is able to give thee much more than this."

There is another important aspect to this interesting part of Amaziah's life. The Israelites (the northern kingdom) were *still* the professed people of God - but God was not with them. The general churches today still profess to be Christians, but God is not with them. Just as Amaziah had to renounce help from the Israelite army, so are we called to be separate, whatever the cost. We are to seek all our help in God.

But, of course, the Israelites did not like it, and neither do the churches today. To them what are we? "Narrow-minded, sitting in judgment," etc. And so the Israelite army, offended, angry, began to pillage and destroy.

The King Who Proved A Disappointment

We are called to be separate from:
secularism
ecumenism
Romanism
modernism

But it will bring opposition and reproach, and sometimes persecution.

But God helped Amaziah, without the Israelites, and he was victorious.

* * *

A SAD CHANGE

But now we find strange things beginning to happen, almost like a landslide in Amaziah's life.

First of all, he showed incredible cruelty following his victory (v. 12). We wonder why?

Next, he adopted the idols of the people he had just conquered, brought them back, and worshipped them (v. 14). Apart from the wickedness of this, the foolishness is incredible - even naturally. Their gods could not help or defend the people Amaziah was fighting against. They were entirely overcome in battle. Yet Amaziah turned to *them* rather than God.

Thirdly, when the prophet came to reprove him for his foolishness and sin, he refused to listen. (We do not know whether this was the *same* prophet who graciously counselled him before, or another.) But Amaziah threatened to kill him. It seems that for some reason or other he had become completely infatuated. The prophet told him in no uncertain terms (v. 16) that all this would end in his destruction.

And then Amaziah foolishly picked a quarrel with the King of Israel in most insulting language (verse 17 and following). There was no need for confrontation. It is always best to avoid open confrontation if scripturally it can be avoided.

Well, Amaziah was completely defeated. "Be not deceived; God is not mocked: for what a man soweth, that shall he also reap."

Verse 25: after this Amaziah lived another fifteen years, but we learn nothing about him good or bad. But verse 27, he was murdered.

Amaziah

The whole account of King Amaziah's life leaves us feeling miserable. He was a great disappointment, and it is very sad when after promising beginnings people prove to be disappointments.

This has often been the case, and it makes the people of God sad. How many ministers have seemed to make very promising beginnings, but then popularity has ruined them, and they have turned aside from the truth. Clergymen who have appeared serious and devout, when appointed bishops, seem to forget their former friends and beliefs.

So the whole account leaves us feeling miserable. It reminds us of a lovely ship embarking with admiring crowds, but soon in the storm being completely wrecked. But there is a voice in all this for us:

1. Be sure you are right in God's sight. Do not take it for granted. Pray that God will make you right and establish you in the truth. The vital thing is to be born again of the Holy Spirit, blessed with repentance and faith, feeling to be nothing in self but trusting only in the blood and righteousness of Jesus.

2. Pray to be kept, for grace to endure, to continue - so that *you* do not prove a disappointment. You will have trials, problems, difficulties, temptations, but

> "Then to maintain the battle
> With soldier-like behaviour;
> To keep the field, and never yield,
> But firmly eye the Saviour ....
> This, this is faith will conquer death,
> And overcome the devil."

THE KING WHO BECAME PROUD

UZZIAH 810 - 758

You can read about Uzziah in 2 Chronicles chapter 26, and in 2 Kings chapter 15, verses 1 to 7.

Usually known as King Uzziah, the Book of Kings calls him Azariah. Uzziah means, "My strength is Jehovah"; Azariah means, "Jehovah helps." It is clear that Uzziah was a good and gracious man.

He became king when he was young, only 16 (2 Chronicles, chapter 26 verse 1), but verse 5, "he sought God," and verse 7, "God helped him." Later we have a very strong expression, "He was marvellously helped."

EXTREME PROSPERITY

Uzziah's prosperity was very great, both nationally and spiritually.
Verses 6, 7, he overthrew the Philistines, the Arabians and the Mehunims.
Verse 8, he reduced Ammon to tribute.
Verse 9, he strengthened the fortifications of Jerusalem.
Verse 10, he improved agriculture.
Verses 11, 12, he reorganised the army.
Verses 14, 15, he introduced engines of war for casting stones.
All this is a wonderful picture of great prosperity.

BUT IN THE TRIAL OF PROSPERITY HE FAILED

In his wonderful work on divine providence John Flavel says that thousands more perish in the trial of prosperity than the trial of adversity. While Uzziah was kept dependent, praying, looking to God, he prospered; all went well. But when he became proud, self-confident, self-reliant, he failed.

There is a warning for us each here. How often we have seen this! A young man has a little family. He is not very well off, he has financial problems, and then there is sickness in the family - but he is wonderfully blessed as he has to pray earnestly to God and depend on Him alone for help. Then relief comes, things are better, and at last he begins to prosper, but what has happened to his religion? He does not give up his outward profession of the Lord's name, he still attends the services, but now he is careless, indifferent, hard, proud, despising others. We do need to beware of this.

Sometimes you see it with a politician. What a good Member of Parliament he is, how helpful to his constituents, but when he becomes a cabinet minister, he becomes aloof, and his old friends are forgotten. You may have experienced this even with some of your old friends; it is very hurtful, but they do not want to know you any more. Very sad this is if it is with a minister of religion.

It is said that Lord Mackay was a notable exception. A poor crofter's son, he achieved the highest office, next only to the Queen, the Lord Chancellor. But he retained his modesty, and even the newspapers commented on it, though they said he had "a brain like five computers."

Watch your spirit in little things. You have problems, difficulties, sorrow. You pray; you are dependent. Then things become easier. But where are you spiritually now?

THE KEY VERSE OF THE CHAPTER
The key verse is:
"He was marvellously helped until he was strong, but when he was strong...."

UZZIAH'S SIN
Uzziah presumed on the priesthood. Was he a child of God? or not? We are clearly told that he *was* a child of God, but we are equally clearly told that he *acted wrongly*. Here we have a child of God falling into sin and dishonouring God. But beware of the two opposites.

The King Who Became Proud

Sometimes a child of God acts wrongly, and some people say, "He cannot be a child of God if he does things like this." And then there are others who say, "He is such a godly man. What he is doing must be right. There must be some reason for it." But in Scripture we often read of a child of God acting wrongly - Abraham, Isaac, Jacob, David, Jonah, etc. They were *not* right in what they did, but they were the children of God. And when God's people act wrongly, then God chastens them, as a loving Father, for their good. No real Christian can sin cheaply.

* * *

The king went into the temple, and tried to perform an act that was only permitted to the priests, that of burning incense. But why not? He was a great man, a famous king. Surely there was no harm in him doing what he did? So King Uzziah must have thought and reasoned. But God was angry, and he was sorely punished - with leprosy.

Verse 17 and following verses: The high priest and eighty other priests withstood the king. They were horrified; they knew he was doing wrong. They rebuked him; they even tried to push him out of the temple; and the Bible calls them "valiant men."

These "valiant men" are of great value in a country and in a church. No one likes to be told they are wrong, especially people in high positions of authority, but our best friends are those who tell us the truth. England needs valiant men today. This has been the great fault with our own royal family. Advisers have fawned; they have been concerned about their own position and reputation. We have not had the valiant men to say, "Charles, you are not treating Diana right!" "Charles, you should not have this affair with Camilla!"

But what about our own lives? Value those who tell you when you are behaving wrongly. They are your best friends.

Of course, in the New Testament we have the example of Priscilla and Aquila. There was this wonderful, new, young minister, Apollos - eloquent, mighty in the Scriptures. What would our churches think of him today? But there was a defect in his preaching, and Priscilla and Aquila discerned it. They knew it was not for his good, nor for the good of the church of God. So what did they do? Whisper to everyone that Apollos was unsound? Or, on the other hand, say, "It is nothing to do with us!" What did they do? They quietly spoke to him; and I do not know whether more to admire the grace in Priscilla and Aquila for the way they behaved, or the grace in Apollos in receiving it. The next we read of Apollos, what a wonderful blessing he was made to the church of God!

However, Uzziah did not like being told he was wrong. He was king. He was angry. But God immediately smote him with leprosy so that he could not get out of the temple quickly enough. He remained a leper till the day of his death, and lived in "a several house" (in isolation), and was cut off from the house of the Lord. Nor could he continue as king; his son Jotham reigned in his stead. A very, very sad end - and this was a godly man. We believe he is now in heaven singing the praises of free grace, for Scripture is clear he was right in God's sight. But how he suffered for his sin!

WHAT WAS UZZIAH'S SIN?

To us the punishment that King Uzziah received seems to be extremely severe. Leprosy in Scripture is often the judgment of God, a loathsome, incurable disease. His latter life was one of disaster. Our natural minds would say, "What a harsh punishment for such a small thing!" What then was Uzziah's sin in burning the incense in the house of the Lord?

1. *Disobedience.* Uzziah clearly disobeyed God's Word which forbade anyone, not of the tribe of Levi, to usurp the office of one of God's priests and burn incense to the Lord. Uzziah thought that, being king, he could break God's laws. It was not ignorance; he should have known better.

In Scripture disobedience is always counted a great sin.

When we were at school, perhaps the teacher told the children that for the time being in no circumstances must anyone leave his place. Immediately, with a grin on his face, a naughty boy walks out of his place. He is punished. His mother comes to school. "It is dreadful. All my son did was to leave his place, and yet he was punished!" "No," says the headmaster, "he was not punished for leaving his place. *He was punished for disobedience!"*

   2. *He destroyed the type.*
This may seem a difficult point to follow, but in the Old Testament there were many types (or figures) of spiritual things which would be made known in Christ. God was very jealous of these types.

   For instance, Moses. He was forbidden to enter the promised land - dear, godly man, even though he pleaded with the Lord. Why? For smiting the rock when God had told him to *speak* to the rock. It seems a great punishment for a small fault. Of course, it was disobedience; but more than that he destroyed the type. Christ, the Rock of ages, is only to be smitten *once* - at Calvary - and every blessing flows from His wounded side, the stream of living water. Henceforth it is, *Speak* to the Rock. The rock had been smitten once by Moses in Rephidim. It must not be smitten a second time. Speak now, and the living water will freely flow. Do not smite the rock a second time or this beautiful type of Christ will be destroyed.

   So it was with Aaron's sons, Nadab and Abihu. They destroyed the type. They offered strange fire, not lit from the altar where the lamb was slain and the blood was shed. They destroyed the type.

   So again with Uzza. He put forth his hand to steady the ark when the oxen stumbled, and immediately died. But surely this was good? This was being helpful? But he destroyed the type. An almighty and holy God does not need weak, sinful hands to hold His ark.

   What was Uzziah's sin? He destroyed the type. No one was to be both *King* AND *Priest* except the Lord Jesus. The type is Melchisedec. There were many kings, and many priests, but no one was to be both. This was reserved for Christ - see Zechariah 6. "*He* shall be a priest upon the throne." The New Testament speaks much of the King - Priest, "even Jesus, made an high priest for ever after the order of Melchisedec."

CONCLUSION
   One of the best known chapters in the Old Testament is Isaiah

chapter 6 where the prophet viewed God's glory and heard the holy seraphims singing, "Holy, holy, holy."

Now how does that chapter begin? *"In the year that King Uzziah died ...."* It was a time of crisis in Judah, a time of sadness for the prophet, the throne of Judah empty, the throne of Judah vacated. But Isaiah saw a throne that will never be empty, the eternal throne of God in heaven. Amid life's changing scenes, may we view that throne, never to be vacated like that of Uzziah. "The Lord sitteth upon the throne, the Lord sitteth king for ever."

The King Who Walked Humbly Before His God

JOTHAM 758 - 742

You can read about Jotham in 2 Kings chapter 15, verses 32 to 38 and 2 Chronicles chapter 27.

As we continue with the lives of the kings, an interesting question may be asked. With all the kings, we have an account in the Book of Kings and also in the Book of Chronicles. Why? Why do we have Chronicles as well as Kings? Some of it seems just repetition.

There are really three answers to this.

1. Chronicles gives a fuller account of the kings of Judah.

2. Chronicles especially traces "the hand of God in history" - religious, not political. So some important things happening at the time are passed by, and other things, which would seem small to worldly eyes, are enlarged upon.

3. There is a similarity with the four Gospels. Why four? There are some things in one that are omitted in another; some things briefly mentioned in one that are enlarged upon in another.

So we come to Jotham. Jotham is one of the very little known characters of the Word of God. We do not know much about him. There are only seven verses about him in Kings, and only nine verses about him in Chronicles. But he was a godly man. We are told that he was "right in the sight of the Lord" (2 Chronicles 27. 2), and this is the one thing that really matters. Not to be great, not to be famous, but to be right in God's sight. And the only way we can be right in God's sight is to be saved by grace, clothed in the righteousness of

Jesus, and washed in His precious blood. Jotham's name means "God is upright (or perfect)."

HIS FATHER AND MOTHER

We are told about his father and mother (verses 1 and 2).

His father, Uzziah, was a good man who sinned. Jotham followed his father's *good* example; he did not follow his *bad* example. Many have made the faults and failings of the saints of God an excuse for *their* failings.

His mother's name was Jerusha. (We cannot help but be reminded of the life of that eminent servant of God, David Brainerd, and his friendship with the young, beautiful and godly daughter of the great Jonathan Edwards, whose name was Jerusha.) It is very noticeable that so often we are told who the king's mother was. A mother can have a tremendous influence on a young child during the early, formative years - for good or evil. (When we read of Ahaziah's wicked mother, Athaliah, we were told that *her* mother was the infamous Jezebel.)

Dr. Philip Doddridge, the well-known Northampton minister and hymnwriter, owed much to his godly mother. Round the fireplace in their home were Dutch tiles with pictures of the Bible stories, and Philip's mother used to tell him these stories and simply explain the truth. He dated his first spiritual impressions from this time. We hope you girls who become mothers will be made a blessing to your children.

THE CRITICS

You will sometimes come across critics of the Bible who make much of seeming discrepancies, and because of this deny its inspiration and infallibility. But there is always an explanation when things do not seem to agree. I often give as an example two postcards I received from two girls in our Sunday school who were on holiday together. Both cards were written the same day, both were posted together, both arrived together. One said, "It is a beautiful day"; the other said, "It is raining." Both were truthful girls! It is easy for you to think of an explanation.

The King Who Walked Humbly Before His God

The length of Jotham's reign has given a field day to the critics. "He reigned sixteen years" (verse 1), but 2 Kings 15. 30 speaks of "the twentieth year of Jotham the son of Uzziah." The obvious explanation seems to be that one account dates his whole reign from his father's death, and the other account, when speaking of an event which took place, dates it from the time he became regent in place of his father when his father was struck with leprosy.

"HE PREPARED HIS WAYS"

We are told very little about Jotham. He built the high gate, he built cities and castles and towers. He fought against the Ammonites and was victorious. But though we are not told much about him, we have a precious gem (verse 6):

"He prepared his ways before the Lord."

This is a vital point in our lives: to prepare (or order as the word means), our ways.

1. The way of life. How we need to be prepared for eternity, for by nature we are not prepared. We need the Lord to make us ready - to be saved by His grace. We need to pray:

> "Prepare me, gracious God,
> To stand before Thy face."

2. A poet says, "May our ordered lives confess the beauty of Thy peace." An *ordered* life glorifies God - not a muddle; not just ordered to gain wealth, prestige, pleasure; but ordered by prayer, by the Word of God, looking to Jesus, depending on Him.

3. A few scriptures speak of this ordered life:

"To him that ordereth his conversation aright will I show the salvation of God" (Psalm 50. 23).

"The steps of a good man are ordered by the Lord, and he delighteth in His way" (Psalm 37. 23).

"Order my steps in Thy Word: and let not any iniquity have dominion over me" (Psalm 119. 133).

4. We need to pray the Lord to prepare (order) our ways:
in the family, in the church, in business
in the way of gracious leading and guidance

Jotham

in our choices and decisions
in trouble
at the beginning of the day, the week, the year
> "Order my footsteps by Thy Word,
> And make my heart sincere."

> "Leave God to order all thy ways,
> And trust in Him, whate'er betide."

> "All my times shall ever be
> Ordered by His wise decree."

So we know little about Jotham, but how important what we do know! There are two other important things to remember.

1. His religion was BEFORE GOD. "He prepared his ways *before the Lord his God*." If we possess the fear of the Lord, which is the beginning of wisdom, this will always give us a religion *before God*. We will live, act, behave, as in His sight. So this will make us real, sincere. There will not be a contradiction between what we are in chapel and what we are in the world, or between what we are at home and what we are when with our friends. We shall remember we are always seen by God.

A little servant girl was asked what difference her religion had made to her. After thinking a moment, she said, "I used to clean up well where everyone can see, but now I clean up just as well where no one will look." This is a religion "before the Lord."

2. We are told "Jotham became mighty." He honoured his God, and his God honoured him.

May we possess Jotham's religion.

THE KING WHO TRUSTED GOD

HEZEKIAH 727 - 698

You can read about Hezekiah in 2 Kings chapters 18, 19 and 20, 2 Chronicles chapters 29, 30, 31 and 32, and Isaiah chapters 36, 37, 38 and 39.

The remarkable thing about Hezekiah is the amount of space devoted to him in the Bible. There is a lot - three chapters in 2 Kings, four chapters in 2 Chronicles, and four chapters in Isaiah. So he must be important. Where a lot of space is devoted to anything in Scripture, watch it; it is always something important. Of course, above everything else we notice that so much in the Gospels is devoted to the death of the Lord Jesus.

So when we come to the life of Hezekiah, we are reminded of the purpose of the Bible; it is not just to recount history. So some famous people and famous events are not even mentioned in the Bible, or have very little about them. On the other hand, some little known people and events have pages devoted to them. What we look at is what has been called "the Christian philosophy of history": God is in control, working out His purpose. So the Bible is a spiritual book with so much about spiritual things.

However, Hezekiah is both an important person *and* has a lot of space devoted to him.

THE MAN WHO TRUSTED GOD

Hezekiah was the greatest of all the kings of Judah. He is preeminently *the man who trusted God*. "He trusted in the Lord God of

Israel....For he clave to the Lord, and departed not from following Him .... And the Lord was with him, and he prospered" (2 Kings 18. 5-7).

Trust in God is a wonderful thing; it is the essence of faith. The great point with us is: do we trust God? - especially in the great matter of our souls, trusting Him for salvation, but also in our day by day providential things. "They that trust in the Lord are as mount Zion, which cannot be moved, but abideth for ever." We may not be able to crystallise our experience so that we can tell it out from beginning to end; but the great point in real religion is a sinner, in repentance and faith, trusting in Christ and in His precious blood.

"When, through grace, in Christ our trust is,
Justice smiles, and asks no more;
He has washed us in His blood;
He has brought us home to God."

John Bunyan, in his classic autobiography *Grace Abounding to the Chief of Sinners*, speaks of how in great distress he was encouraged by the words: "Did any ever trust in the Lord and were put to shame?" This has always been a help, an encouragement to me. The Lord has never, never failed me when I have been helped to trust in Him.

PROSPERITY: A GOOD START

Hezekiah's was a most wonderful and remarkable reign. His father was a very wicked man who had died at the age of 36, leaving Judah in a dreadful condition in every way. The kingdom of Judah seemed on the point of being wiped out; but under Hezekiah there was a wonderful revival - national and spiritual; a glorious reformation in religion; the cleansing of the temple; the extermination of idolatry. We read of a remarkable thanksgiving day, so that there was scarcely any other like it.

What can one man do? What can one man *not* do if God is with him?

We think of the scripture: "Righteousness exalteth a nation, but sin is a reproach to any people." At present Britain is in the *second* half of the verse: our sin is a reproach. We do not want to be legal - we certainly do not want the "prosperity gospel" popular in the U.S.A. -

but throughout history, when a country has honoured the Lord, the Lord has prospered that country. We think of Queen Victoria who, when asked by an Indian prince, "What is the secret of England's greatness?" showed him an open Bible. We also think of the days of Oliver Cromwell when England was so feared that it is said that Mazarin, the French prime minister, turned pale at the mention of Cromwell's name.

There is a very important verse concerning the beginning of Hezekiah's reign and his reforms (2 Chronicles 29. 3): "He *in the first year of his reign, in the first month,* opened the doors of the house of the Lord, and repaired them." He started as he meant to continue - *right at the very beginning.*

Always begin as you mean to go on. Those of you who are hoping to be married, begin as you mean to go on. Do not say, "We will wait till we have settled down and got things straight." Begin as you mean to go on - family prayer right from the first day; attending the week evening prayer meeting as soon as you are back from your honeymoon.

If you start a new school, or college, or a new job, start as you mean to continue. Let them know what you believe. Let them know where you stand - right from the start. If you do not, it will be hard to make a stand later. Let them know you keep Sunday as the Lord's day; that you go to chapel; that you cannot go with them to the pub, or join in their worldly activities. (For example, not some half-hearted suggestion that it is not convenient *this* Sunday.) *Start as you mean to go on.*

NOTE: It was during Hezekiah's prosperous reign that the ten tribes were taken into Assyrian captivity, and so Israel, the northern kingdom, virtually came to an end. God was faithful to His threatenings by the prophets.

There were three outstanding events in Hezekiah's life.

I. SENNACHERIB AND THE SIEGE OF JERUSALEM
Though Hezekiah honoured his God, this did not save him from trouble. Often God's people, when walking tenderly before Him,

come into real trouble. And this was *real* trouble. Sennacherib and his mighty army surrounded Jerusalem. It seemed certain death and destruction; there was no way of escape. But Hezekiah trusted God, and God honoured his faith. His prayer was answered and a miracle was performed.

There are a number of important and interesting principles which are very helpful to young people who fear God.

1. Rabshakeh, Sennacherib's messenger, came with dreadful threats and blasphemies. One challenge he gave was:
"WHAT CONFIDENCE IS THIS WHEREIN THOU TRUSTEST?" (2 Kings 18. 19). And Hezekiah knew the answer! It is a great mercy if we do - where we are looking, where we are trusting.

"Other refuge have I none,
Hangs my helpless soul on Thee."

2. Another thing. Rabshakeh said God had told him to come. "Am I now come up without the Lord against this place to destroy it? *The Lord said to me*, Go up against this land, and destroy it" (2 Kings 18. 25).

Sometimes people will tell you that they have a clear word from God, that God has told them to do something. And sometimes it happens that it intimately concerns you, and you are not happy.

For instance, what happens when a man says the Lord has told him to preach, and his church cannot receive him? Or again, more than once I have had girls come to see me, deeply distressed, because boys whom they accounted godly had told them that they had a clear word from God to marry them. My answer has been that this is unfair. I asked them, "Do you love him? If you do not love him, you cannot marry him, whatever he says."

We are reminded of the well-known story concerning the eccentric eighteenth century minister, John Berridge. A lady came and told him she had a clear word from the Lord to marry him. After a moment's thought, Berridge replied, "As it concerns me so intimately, I think the Lord would have told me also." This may make us smile - but it is good divinity!

3. Verse 36: "The people held their peace, and answered him not a word: for the king's commandment was, saying, Answer him not."

THE KING WHO TRUSTED GOD

There is a time to speak, and a time to be silent. We need the Lord to show us which time it is. God's people and Hezekiah their king here were silent to Rabshakeh, but *they were not silent to God.*

I once preached in a Cambridgeshire village. The deacon, during the week, had received a difficult, insulting letter, and had prayed for guidance on the Lord's day how to answer it. Strangely for me, my text was one word: "SILENCE."

Sometimes we are to "answer a fool according to his folly" by being silent.

4. In chapter 19, verse 14, Hezekiah received a threatening letter: "And Hezekiah went up into the house of the Lord, and spread it before the Lord."

It is wise counsel to spread our letters before the Lord in prayer - both letters we write *before* writing them and *before* posting them, and letters we have received before answering them. We do not need, like Hezekiah, literally to go to chapel to spread the letter before the Lord; this was the old dispensation. We can spread the letter before the Lord where we are - sometimes just "the upward glancing of an eye, when none but God is near."

If you have an important letter to write, spread it before the Lord. If when you have written it, you have any degree of uncertainty, leave it till the next day before posting. When the next day comes, you may find that you tear the letter up; you go straight to the post; or you alter a few words or a sentence.

Two or three years ago I spoke about Hezekiah spreading his letter before the Lord. A young man had in his pocket a letter he had written to a young lady asking her to go out with him. He was afraid of sending it, so delayed till after the service. After spreading it before the Lord he posted it that day. The answer was, Yes! And I was invited to be a guest at the wedding.

HEZEKIAH'S PRAYER

After this Hezekiah prayed, and his prayer is recorded in 2 Kings 19. 15-19. This is a beautiful prayer ("a pattern prayer") and it received a good answer.

1. Hezekiah viewed the mercy seat. "O Lord God of Israel, which

dwellest between the cherubims" - that is where the mercy seat was. This is the ground and foundation of all real prayer, the mercy seat sprinkled with blood (the type so beautifully fulfilled in the Lord Jesus Christ).

> "That rich atoning blood,
> Which, sprinkled round, I see,
> Provides for those who come to God
> An all-prevailing plea."

We are sinful and unworthy; we do not deserve our prayers to be answered. It is through the Person, name and blood of Jesus that our poor prayers ascend to heaven, and receive blessed answers. Hezekiah's did here.

2. Hezekiah saw that God is in control. "Thou art the God, even Thou alone, of all the kingdoms of the earth." It is not Sennacherib who is in control, not Satan; it is *God*. *He* is on the throne.

3. Hezekiah saw that God is almighty. "Thou hast made heaven and earth." Nothing is impossible with God. The hardest thing is easy.

4. Hezekiah made his petition known. It was a simple, definite one: "Save Thou us."

God performed a miracle in answering this prayer. The next day (or soon after) round the walls of Jerusalem were 185,000 dead bodies - the mighty Assyrian army.

This is one of the greatest miracles in the Old Testament. It can only be compared with the overthrow of the Egyptians on the banks of the Red Sea. God did it all. Hezekiah needed to do nothing.

II. HEZEKIAH'S SICKNESS AND RECOVERY

This was another great trial in the life of Hezekiah, and another wonderful answer to prayer.

One day, when he was "sick unto death," the prophet came to him with the alarming news: "Thou shalt die, and not live; set thine house in order." It was a terrible shock to Hezekiah. He did not feel ready. I wonder how you and I would feel if the news suddenly came to us that we were soon to die. I remember one young lady who had cancer. When she was told she could not live above three months, she thought a moment, and then said, "No cause for tears when you receive the King's invitation!"

But there was something else: he had no son and heir. If he died without a child, what of the royal line, the promise of Messiah as a son of David? But now David's line was to die out. No heir - no Messiah - no Saviour! Some people have thought that Isaiah's prayer at this time, recorded in Isaiah 38, uses very extravagant language - but this was the reason.

We are told that Hezekiah "turned his face to the wall" (2 Kings 20. 2). He turned away from everyone and everything, and cast himself completely on his God. This is a terrible experience at times for God's people - no way out, no way of escape, no way in which it seems that even God can deliver. But in looking back it is a blessed experience.

Isaiah 38, which includes Hezekiah's prayer, is a most remarkable chapter. No chapter in all the Bible contains a greater contrast: the sheer misery of the first half; the sheer delight of the second half. And in the middle, like a bridge from one to the other, is a little prayer: "O Lord; I am oppressed: undertake for me." And that prayer was answered.

It was a desperate prayer, seemingly against what God has foretold: "Thou shalt die." Joseph Hart wrote a hymn on this whole subject, and at this point says:

"Can prayer reverse the stern decree?
It may; at least I'll try."

Many people have testified what a help those two lines have been to them.

The prayer was answered; God said he would live another fifteen years (during which time a son and heir was born). A miracle was performed, and he was cured in three days. Most wonderfully a sign of his complete recovery and prolonged life was given: the sun dial of Ahaz, which no doubt the king could see from his palace, would go *back* ten degrees - perhaps that means from noon to seven o'clock in the morning. God holds all creation in His hands, and even the sun obeys His decree. Never has there been such a thing before or since. What things God will do for the comfort of His people!

But it is very interesting. Though Hezekiah's complete cure was promised, and that it would be quick, he still had to put a plaster of figs on the boil (cancer?). God works by means. We are not to be fatalists. We are not to *trust* in doctors but we are not to *neglect* them. The feeblest means, with God's blessing, will work; the best, without God's blessing, will not.

What about when God promises (or threatens) something, and then it does not come to pass?

We have a clear case of this here with Hezekiah. God told him he was to die. He did not.

Perhaps the case of Jonah and Nineveh is the best way to explain this. God said, "Forty days, and Nineveh shall be destroyed." But Nineveh was *not* destroyed. Was God wrong?

God's threatening always implies that this will take place *if there is no repentance or prayer*. Sometimes this is stated, sometimes not. (See so many of God's threatenings in the minor prophets.) For instance, we say, "The wicked will go to hell." That is true; but we always imply "if they are not blessed with repentance." Nineveh repented, and prayed to God, and so was spared.

It was exactly the same with Hezekiah here - so the threat was averted.

There is a sad end to this story. A wonderful miracle, a wonderful answer to prayer, but "Hezekiah rendered not again according to the benefit done unto him" (2 Chronicles 32. 25). You would have thought he would have been overwhelmed with gratitude, but he was not. And we are often the same, aren't we? One of our great sins is base ingratitude. How we need to watch this! How often we are guilty! We soon forget; we take God's mercies for granted.

III. THE VISIT OF THE AMBASSADORS

The Bible is different from every other book. All other books hide the faults and failings of their heroes, but the Bible does not. But even if they do mention any sin, it is usually not at the end but rather the life story ends in a wonderful crescendo (just as we were told to plan our essays at school - not an anticlimax at the end!).

The last thing we hear of Hezekiah is sad. He was blessed with honour and riches in abundance, but he fell through pride. Pride seems to be a sin which slips in anywhere, where other sins dare not enter. After Hezekiah's recovery from his illness, the mighty King of Babylon sent a present and letter of congratulations. And Hezekiah was flattered. Beware of flattery! What did he do? Show them all the wonderful treasures he possessed, his beautiful house; "there was nothing in his house, nor in all his dominion, that Hezekiah showed them not."

Hezekiah was very pleased with all that he had shown to the ambassadors from Babylon, but God was not pleased. He sent Isaiah the prophet to reprove Hezekiah. The question he asked is very important for us:

"WHAT HAVE THEY SEEN IN THY HOUSE?" What kind of things do people see in our homes? Are they things that honour God, or like the television, that dishonour Him?

Hezekiah was honest. He did not make excuses. But God told him that before long, *all* the precious things in the king's house would be carried away, including his descendants. Hezekiah had grace to say, "Good is the word of the Lord."

So the story of Hezekiah ends on a sad note. Why? He was Judah's greatest king. Because we are to remember that the best of men are only men at best (and fallen men). Across the lives even of the most godly is that word written: "Where sin abounded, grace did much more abound."

THE MOST WICKED KING

MANASSEH 698 - 643

You can read about Manasseh in 2 Kings chapter 21, and 2 Chronicles chapter 33.

Before coming to Manasseh, let us make again the point made at the very beginning. What have all these old kings to do with us? We have our problems, our difficulties; we are entering "the millennium". Surely these old kings have nothing to do with us? They have *everything* to do with us! Man is the same; God is the same; our needs are the same; God's answers are the same. So we come to Manasseh.

HIS SIN

There was never a more wicked man than Manasseh, and yet he obtained mercy. One of the beautiful hymns we sing about the blood of Jesus ends:

> "That sacred flood, from Jesus' veins,
>   Is free to take away
> A Mary's or Manasseh's stains,
>   Or sins more vile than they."

Manasseh's birth was remarkable; he was twelve when his father died, and fifteen years before, Hezekiah had been told he was about to die. But his life was lengthened out - so Manasseh was a child of prayer and a child of promise. Yet when he became king he began to practise most abominable wickedness. He was guilty of:

> idolatry - even in the temple
> star worship

The Most Wicked King

unbelievable cruelty - he sacrificed his children to Moloch; he made the streets of Jerusalem run with blood; he is believed to have had Isaiah the prophet sawn in two.

Godly prophets were sent to reprove and warn him - Joel, Naham, Habakkuk, Isaiah - but he would not listen. It is recorded that he sinned "above the Ammonites"; what the heathen were guilty of is much worse in an Israelite.

Where did all the wicked people come from at the beginning of his reign?

In the days of Hezekiah Judah appeared a most godly nation, but as soon as he died there was wickedness on every hand. It reminds us of the reign of Charles II, King of England (1660-1685), whose reign was notorious for profligacy and evil. Yet he became king following the death of Oliver Cromwell and the Puritans, "the rule of the saints." The only explanation is that there must have been a terrible lot of formality and hypocrisy during the Cromwell period, and when things were changed men and women came out in their true colours. The well known song "The Vicar of Bray" dates from this period: whoever was in power - the Roman Catholics, the Church of England, the Presbyterians, the Church of England again - he was determined still to retain his living and remain as vicar! It must have been exactly the same when Manasseh succeeded his father Hezekiah as king.

Nowadays, I suppose, we would speak of "peer pressure" - a dangerous thing.

Manasseh had a very godly father. Surely no parent can have a greater sorrow than to see a child of many prayers running recklessly in the ways of wickedness. Grace does not run in the blood though often it runs in families - and we can see much mercy in this. Some of us can trace a work of grace in at least six succeeding generations. But it is not automatic! Beware of trusting in your parents' prayers, and *do* beware of any people saying they "have a word" about you.

I knew an old man who lived much of his life in sin and spiritual unconcern. He had a very godly wife, and presumed that her prayers for him must be answered and so he would get to heaven at last. One day she said to him, "Ben, I can't pray for you any longer! I am never going to pray for you again!" And it came like an arrow into his heart.

He now had to pray for himself, and he found no peace till he found peace with God. *We need a personal religion.*

HIS REPENTANCE

Manasseh was wonderfully changed by the sovereign, free, abounding grace of God.

It was in affliction. He was taken a prisoner and then led to Babylon in chains. There God blessed him with true repentance, and true repentance always leads to forgiveness. Do not pray for trouble, but when it comes, do seek that it may be profitable to you. How often God speaks through trouble; trouble has a voice!

"When he was in affliction, he besought the Lord his God, and humbled himself greatly before the God of his fathers, and prayed unto Him: and He was intreated of him, and heard his supplication, and brought him again to Jerusalem into his kingdom. Then Manasseh knew that the Lord He was God" (2 Chronicles 33, verses 12, 13).

How do we know that Manasseh's repentance was genuine?

1. His prayer. He became a man of prayer. Though not given in the Bible, his reputed prayer is given by Matthew Henry the commentator (taken from the apocrypha books entitled "The prayer of Manasses, king of Judah, when he was holden captive in Babylon"). In it he "gives glory to God as the God of their fathers and their righteous seed, as the Creator of the world, a God whose anger is insupportable, and yet His merciful promise unmeasurable." He pleads that God has "promised repentance and forgiveness to those that have sinned, and has appointed repentance unto sinners, that they may be saved - not just to Abraham, Isaac and Jacob, but to me that am a sinner; for I have sinned above the number of the sands of the sea. Forgive me, O Lord, forgive me, and destroy me not. Thou art the God of those that repent." He ends: "Therefore I will praise Thee for ever." 2. The complete change in his life. How he tried to put things right that he had put wrong! He restored the temple; he put down idolatry; he got rid of all that was evil. Remarkably God restored his kingdom to him.

The Most Wicked King

"*No man liveth to himself.*"

Manasseh's evil influence had corrupted many. Now he sought that his gracious influence might affect many. But he could not completely eradicate the evil he had encouraged.

We are reminded of John Newton, author of "How sweet the name of Jesus sounds!" As a godly minister he spoke solemnly to a person about his atheism and blasphemy, only to be told that many years before he had learned it from Newton himself when he had been an atheist and blasphemer.

We are also reminded of the criminal about to be hanged, who railed against his father and mother for permitting him to go in evil ways.

Above all we are reminded that Manasseh's own son, Amon, lived and died in his sin.

REPENTANCE

Repentance is one of the great truths of the gospel. It is the gift of God. There is no salvation without it. Repentance is always joined with faith. An old minister asked, "What is repentance?" He then turned round completely in the pulpit with his back to the congregation. Repentance is a complete turning round - from sin, the world, our past life; to Christ.

With repentance is inward sorrow for sin and humble confession, and also an outward change of life. Manasseh had both. Remember the children's hymn:

> "Repentance is to leave
> The sins we did before,
> And show that we in earnest grieve
> By doing them no more."

God has promised that all who truly repent and believe on His Son, the Lord Jesus Christ, will be forgiven. It is on mercy's ground, through the blood of Christ, that repenting sinners are forgiven.

* * *

A remarkable story is told of a famous minister in the Highlands of

Scotland, Hector M'Phail, who died in 1774. He was the minister in the well-known tale of "The Highland Kitchen Maid." The story is as follows:

In his last years Hector M'Phail was often cast down and tried. Feeling very dejected he fell asleep and dreamed that he was waiting, lonely and dejected, outside the gate of heaven. The gate was closed and, having none to help him, he lay down to die.

Suddenly he heard footsteps approaching and, looking up, recognised Noah, Abraham and the patriarchs. As they drew near, the gate of heaven flew open, and to shouts of triumph, they entered. But there he lay helpless and hopeless.

Soon he heard more footsteps, and this time recognised Moses, Aaron, Samuel, David and the prophets, and again the gate flew open, and there was a joyful entry. Yet he himself was left outside.

A third company approaching, he recognised the apostles and some early Christians and watched them enter with rejoicing like the others - himself with less hope than ever.

A fourth company appeared with Luther and Knox at the head. Passing him by, they too had an abundant entry into the city.

But again he sees yet a fifth company, those he had known and loved who had died in the Lord, but though they passed very close, he dare not venture to join them. Now as the gate closed, he lay down to die in despair.

But all at once he sees a lonely pilgrim, and recognises him as Manasseh, "the chief of sinners." Laying hold of his skirt, he creeps behind him and sees the gate open and the glory of heaven shining on his face. Waking up, the words remained with him:

"This is a faithful saying, and worthy of all acceptation, that Christ Jesus came into the world to save sinners, of whom I am chief."

The King Who Obeyed God's Word

JOSIAH 641 - 610

You can read about King Josiah in 2 Kings chapters 22 and 23, and 2 Chronicles chapters 34 and 35.

Josiah was one of the most godly of all the kings - perhaps *the* most godly. We are told "there was none like him." In many ways he was superior to David; he did not have the same sins and failures.

Josiah was only 8 when he began to reign, and he was 39 when he died, having been king for 31 years. In British history, in Tudor times, we had a young, godly king Edward VI, and he became known as "the English Josiah." He was only 16 when he died.

It is remarkable that Josiah had a most ungodly father, Amon, who reigned only two years, and yet he himself was so different. It must be exceedingly difficult for a boy or girl blessed with grace to live in an ungodly home. Many of us know an old lady who, when she was baptized as a girl, was told by her mother, "If you are baptized, you do not come back to live here!" (In the old magazines we even read of people being threatened with death when they came home from being baptized.) Sometimes grace is found in the most unexpected places and, though painful, grace will prevail against all opposition and persecution.

Mention is made of Josiah's mother - as we have noticed again and again with the kings. Maybe she had a gracious influence. Mothers have a wonderful opportunity for good or evil in training their little children. Many people have traced their first spiritual impressions right back to something they heard at their mother's knee. Praying mothers are a great blessing.

JOSIAH

Very remarkably, Josiah was prophesied of *by name* over 300 years before he was born. This was when God sent a prophet to reprove the idolatry of Jeroboam, the first king of the northern kingdom of the ten tribes. The prophet cried, "O altar, altar, thus saith the Lord; Behold, a child shall be born unto the house of David, *Josiah by name*; and upon thee shall he offer the priests of the high places that burn incense upon thee, and men's bones shall be burnt upon thee" (1 Kings 13. 2). There is only one other person prophesied of *by name* in the prophets, Cyrus. It is a clear evidence that Scripture is inspired when the Lord foretells things which will take place, often in great detail, many years before they happen, and specially remarkable when a person's *name* is actually mentioned.

JOSIAH'S REFORMS

Very early Josiah began to seek the Lord. We are told that this was in the eighth year of his reign, that is, when he would be 15. No one is too young to seek the Saviour, and He has promised that all who seek Him shall find. He has said, "I love them that love Me, and those that seek Me early shall find Me."

God's grace will always have a sanctifying effect on our hearts. If a person is blessed with grace, then this will always be seen in his behaviour. So we see Josiah acting, doing many things. Josiah, with God's help, sought to reform the kingdom.

1. Even in the house of the Lord there were vessels for Baal and Ashteroth. Josiah purged the temple of all idol worship (2 Kings 23. 4-7).

2. Just at the entering in of the temple there were stables for horses "for the sun." Josiah took them away (verses 11-12).

3. He broke down the houses of the sodomites that were close to the house of the Lord (verse 7). This is very much a present day issue. "Sodomites" is the old word for "homosexuals," and we find God's Word is very clear against it both in the Old and New Testaments. It is not a matter of our feelings or opinions or what we think. The question is: has God made known His mind? Most certainly He has.

4. Josiah cleansed all the idols from Jerusalem, and put down the "high places" in the land (verse 5).

The King Who Obeyed God's Word

5. He defiled the valley of Topheth, putting an end to all Molech worship (verse 10). (This was incredibly cruel, involving child sacrifice.)
6. Idolatrous priests, conjurors and wizards were removed.
7. Josiah carried his reforms up into the northern kingdom of Israel, the ten tribes (verses 15-18). This kingdom had now been overcome by the Assyrians and so, as a kingdom, was at an end. Here he broke down the altar of Jeroboam at Bethel - thus fulfilling that remarkable prophecy made over 300 years before he was born.
8. He thoroughly repaired the temple of the Lord.

All this was a result of the grace of God working in Josiah's heart and the constraint of love to the Lord.

(It is not clear how much of this was *before* the discovery of God's law and how much *after*. Kings suggests *after*, Chronicles *before*.)

Good works

If a person is blessed with grace, there will always be an effect. This is something which is very much lacking in much present day religion - yet the Lord Jesus emphasised it: "By their *fruits* ye shall know them." What good is an apple tree if in the autumn there are no apples on the branches, or only sour ones?

It is very foolish (and ignorant) when people say, "We do not believe in good works!" We *do* believe in good works - not as the vital root but the fruit on the bough; not as the foundation on which our hope is built; not *for* salvation but flowing *from* salvation.

In my early days I spoke at Hope Chapel, Rochdale, and in my youthful zeal kept saying, "We have *nothing* to do! We have *nothing* to do!" An aged deacon, who had been a pillar in the church there since Jabez Eddison's days, quietly said to me afterwards, with a smile, "I understand exactly what you mean, but as an old man I find I have so much to do!" And he began to speak of prayer, mortifying the flesh, wrestling with sin and Satan, etc - almost an exposition of Colossians chapter 3!

REPAIRING THE HOUSE OF GOD

Love to the Lord will always be shown in love to His house. Some of us look back to our early days when we *longed* for the Lord's day to come so we could be found in the Lord's house. We could say, "Lord, I have loved the habitation of Thy house, and the place where Thine honour dwelleth."

So it is not surprising that we find King Josiah repairing the temple. And what a wonderful account we have of the workmen! It seems that no accounts had to be kept; they worked "faithfully." They were not "clock watchers"; they gladly did overtime without pay! They just took what money they were entitled to. There is a lovely picture here. What a difference when people act in the fear of God! There is a most important principle here concerning *our* work. How do we work? - not just for God's people but even for an ungodly employer.

A remarkable discovery

Whilst the men were at work in the temple, they made an amazing discovery. *The book of God's holy law was found, hidden among the rubbish.* Perhaps this was the original (it would be the five books of Moses), or perhaps a copy - but it appeared to be the *only* copy. The exclamation was, "I have found the book of the law in the house of the Lord." How strange! But how typical of so many churches today! GOD'S WORD LOST IN GOD'S HOUSE.

One thing that astounds us - how much godliness and grace King Josiah had when he, like everyone else, knew so little of God's Word. Yet over the years there have been many accounts of how people have been convicted or blessed through just a "snippet" of God's Word they have come across. One person in deep sorrow of soul found just one verse: "The blood of Jesus Christ His Son cleanseth us from all sin."

Immediately the Book was taken to the king and read to him. He was distraught. He saw that there were so many things wrong with himself personally, and also in his kingdom. We are reminded of the scripture: "By the law is the knowledge of sin." This is what happens when a person is born again: God's Word shows him where he is wrong, so that he feels his need of a Saviour.

How long is it since God's Word put something right that was wrong in *your* life? Was it something you had to give up? Or was it something that you were not doing but now you knew you should? We are reminded of the story of the woman who said she had heard the most remarkable sermon she had ever heard. She could not remember the text, or the subject, but when asked why it was so remarkable, she replied, "You know I have a little shop. No one knew but some of my weights for the scales were 'light weights.' As soon as the service ended, I had to hurry home and get rid of them all!"

So Josiah, deeply saddened on reading the law of God, deeply condemned, sent to "the prophetess Huldah." (We wonder why ever a prophetess? Was it because of the low state of religion into which Judah had sunk?) Her reply was very solemn and yet very blessed. God would bring evil upon Jerusalem, even as the Book of the Law had said. A list of their sins was mentioned, forsaking God, provoking Him to anger. But there was mercy for Josiah.

"But to the King of Judah which sent you to enquire of the Lord, thus shall ye say to him, Thus saith the Lord God of Israel, As touching the words which thou hast heard; because thine heart was tender, and thou hast humbled thyself before the Lord, when thou heardest what I spake against this place, and against the inhabitants thereof, that they should become a desolation and a curse, and hast rent thy clothes, and wept before Me; I also have heard thee, saith the Lord. Behold therefore, I will gather thee unto thy fathers and thou shalt be gathered into thy grave in peace; and thine eyes shall not see all the evil which I will bring upon this place" (2 Kings 22. 18-20).

This verse tells us what a child of God is.
We have a description of Josiah's spiritual character, but these are always the marks of the new birth:
1. tenderness of heart: a heart made soft in the fear of the Lord.
2. humility before God.
3. real repentance.

So whatever happened to Jerusalem, whatever happened to Judah, Josiah would go to heaven when he died. What shall we say about Josiah "coming to his grave in peace"? He was killed in battle! God's thoughts are very different from our thoughts concerning "a peaceful death." Some of God's people have died cruel deaths: eaten by wild beasts, burned at the stake, etc. But they all "come to the grave in peace," everlasting peace for ever. How different the seemingly peaceful death of the wicked!

IF THERE WAS THIS REFORMATION IN JOSIAH'S LIFE, WHY WAS THE KINGDOM OF JUDAH NOT SPARED?

1. Much of the reformation appears to have been only outward, some even hypocritical. It was the work of the king alone; the people generally remained unrepentant.

2. 2 Kings 23. 26 gives the solemn answer. They had filled up the measure of their iniquity: "Notwithstanding the Lord turned not from the fierceness of His great wrath, wherewith His anger was kindled against Judah, because of all the provocations that Manasseh had provoked Him withal." Though King Manasseh himself had repented, the kingdom was too far gone, and iniquity prevailed.

AFTER THE DEATH OF JOSIAH, THE KINGDOM OF JUDAH LASTED ONLY 22 YEARS. JERUSALEM WAS DESTROYED, AND THE PEOPLE CARRIED INTO CAPTIVITY.

AFTER THE DEATH OF JOSIAH, NOTHING GOOD IS MENTIONED OF THE KINGDOM OF JUDAH.

It just remains to mention the account we have of a most solemn keeping of the Passover toward the end of Josiah's reign. It seems that this had been neglected for many years, but now the book of the law had been found, Josiah realised it was wrong not to keep the Passover. So there was this remarkable Passover; "there was none like it" - which seems to mean the exactness with which it was kept in obedience to God's Word. (This seems to have been the great point in Josiah's religion; he wanted *everything* to be governed by God's Word.)

It is exceedingly important, especially concerning our churches and congregations, that everything should be done according to God's Word. I once knew what seemed to be a wonderful chapel but, looking back, there were a few things not according to Scripture. Finally it fell right away. If Scripture is not our standard, then we can drift to the right hand or to the left.

JOSIAH'S DEATH

At the end of his life, still only young, Josiah acted foolishly. We do not know why. Egypt was going to war against Assyria. It had nothing to do with King Josiah or the kingdom of Judah - yet Josiah, despite being warned, went to battle against the King of Egypt, and was killed in battle.

"And Jeremiah lamented for Josiah: and all the singing men and the singing women spake of Josiah in their lamentations to this day" (2 Chronicles 35. 25). There never was such mourning.

* * *

There is a remarkable reference to this, the death of Josiah, Megiddo where he was slain, and the tremendous grief and sorrow. (In our own day we have witnessed the grief following the death of Princess Diana.) The sudden death of the young king in battle must have touched the nation's heart.

In Zechariah chapter 12 the prophet speaks of the great day when God will pour on Jerusalem "the spirit of grace and of supplications: and they shall look upon Me whom they have pierced, and they shall mourn for Him." Then (in verse 11) the prophet says that this mourning will be with *great* bitterness and he can only compare it to the mourning in Judah when Josiah died, "the mourning of Hadadrimmon in the valley of Megiddon."

So with the death of King Josiah, and the approaching end of his kingdom, we are reminded of Him who is King of kings and Lord of lords, and yet in Jerusalem wore a crown of thorns. We have looked at all these Old Testament kings. May we look by faith with repentance to Jesus, and at Calvary mourn "as in the valley of Megiddon," yet find here our hope, our salvation, our heaven. And may we see the head once crowned with thorns now for ever crowned with glory.

"But we see Jesus, who was made a little lower than the angels for the suffering of death, crowned with glory and honour." Let our last thoughts be of Him.

SOME OTHER TITLES BY THE AUTHOR

Bible Doctrines Simply Explained
A simple presentation of Christian doctrine.

Christmas Evans
Welsh evangelist of 18th century.

Miracles of Jesus
More Miracles of Jesus
Parables of Jesus
More Parables of Jesus
People Jesus Met
The Birth of Jesus
The Resurrection of Jesus
A series of books of Bible stories simply retold and illustrated for young children.

Stranger Than Fiction
The Life of William Kiffin, 17th century preacher and M.P.

Six Remarkable Ministers
How God made them to be ministers of the gospel.

Divine Guidance
How may I know God's will?

The Puritan Samson
The Life of David Crosley, 17th century Lancashire preacher.

Through Cloud and Sunshine
Four generations of faithful witness - the Stennett family.

For a full list of publications please write to:

Gospel Standard Trust Publications
12(b) Roundwood Lane
Harpenden
Herts, AL5 3DD
England.